Seung H-Sang Document

Seung H-Sang Document

Youlhwadang **B**

Preface

The architecture introduced in this book is part of the work I have conducted over the last quarter century. Including the 15 years I worked for Kim Swoo Geun, that makes more than 40 years of a career in architecture, or long enough to call it a 'lifelong career'. Yet even now, I cannot always be confident about my work as an architect. I always find my fingers hesitatingly on the drawing deep into the night. What's worse, the result of my countless hours of pain and hesitation so often turns out to be so unsatisfactory to me. Hence I am always embarrassed to announce the completion of a project to the general public. That is why over the past years I have preferred to stay away from architecture magazines. I knew of course that I should not have behaved that way. As one who believes that the work of an architect belongs to the public rather than a handful of individuals, I should live up to this belief and let my work be judged by the public. That was the urge, the sense of responsibility that pushed me to release this book.

I had to call this book a design document rather than a portfolio or collection of my work. I believe architecture is about the reorganization of the life of those who live in the building based on my respect and love for them. Being a record of such work, I would never call this book a portfolio. Another reason is that this book comes in the format of a catalogue. Moreover, I tried to explain the projects in the book from my present point of view. To pay due respect to the readers, it would not be right to just collect my work. Thus, I ended up being defensive and regretful for which I feel embarrassed.

I believe that architecture is the fruit of its process. Although I am always under fire by clients complaining about how particular I am, there is no other way around it. I want to ensure the peace and inherent dignity of life for those who live inside the buildings I design. At the same time, I am sorry but always grateful for their understanding. If this book deserves any praise, it should go to them, and not to me. I express my sincere gratitude to Youlhwadang, who wholeheartedly supported this book.

Seung H-Sang

Photo Credits

Kwon Tae-Gyun 41; Kim Jong Oh 45, 49-51, 53-55, 57-59, 61-63,
65-67, 69-71, 73-75, 77-79, 82-85, 87, 89, 91, 95-97, 99-103,
105-107, 109-111, 113-115, 117-119, 121-123, 125-127, 129-131,
133-137, 139-141, 143-145, 147-149, 151-153, 155; Osamu Murai
12-27, 29-33; Moon Jungsik 35-39; SOHO China 46, 47; Seung
H-Sang 81, 88; IROJE 93, 159, 162; C3 (Kim Jong Oh) 11, 43

Contents

Document   Architecture

Sujoldang

Seoul

1992

Sujoldang is a house that expounds the virtue of simplicity over technique. While the client's only requirement was to build the house inexpensively, as he was a famous historian of Korean art, I implicitly understood that the house should reflect the beauty of Korea. The neighborhood, however, was filled with typical jerry-builder's houses; the houses stood next to each other rather than creating a living community. It consisted of detached 'French style' two-story houses placed in the middle of a fenced rectangular lot with a green lawn on the rest of the plot. This is an arrangement completely out of touch with the way of living that had been in place for thousands of years. Korean society became intoxicated on the Western approach to the house as a building. Even in the early 1990's, the challenge of reconnecting with the tradition of the Korean house lay heavy on the minds of the architectural community. It is my belief that the house should be a space, not a building.

In the small plot of just 230m², I created three courtyards. The floor level of the central courtyard and the living room were made identical in order to blur the lines between the inside and outside. Including this central courtyard, I surrounded all three courtyards with buildings and walls. As a result, the rooms were separated, some only accessible from the exterior. It is an uncomfortable house. However, the inconvenience leads to introspection, which creates harmony within the family, and in the end, makes life better. Some critics have said that the house maintained a good balance between the traditional and modern values of Korea.

Some say that this comes from the harmony between the traditional paper doors, roof tile fences, and modern materials. I respectfully disagree. The feeling of continuity comes from the invisible creation of spaces. At the time, I had just taken up the idea of 'The Beauty of Poverty'. It paved my way as an architect. Sujoldang is the starting point from which I look back to measure how far I have come.

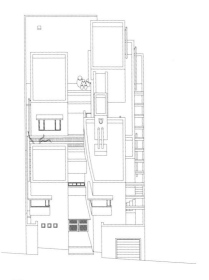

Subaekdang

Namyangju, Gyeonggi-do

1998

Located in the outskirts of Seoul, the house has mountains to the rear and overlooks the vast scenery towards the south. Because the size of the site was ample, the footprint of the house had to be clearly established. The existing embankment divided the land into two parts, and I set a 30m by 15m square area as its framework. Twelve rooms are divided within the space.

Overall, in our traditional houses, the rooms do not serve a purpose. Based on their relative location, the rooms are simply called main room, the opposite room, or hall room. The room can become a dining space when a dining table is set, a bedroom when bed sheets are laid out, a study when a desk is provided. In the Korean house, the use of the room changes according to our wishes. But with the influence of Western housing popularized in the 1970's, beds were placed in the bedroom, and the dining table occupied the dining room. This changed our lives, altering our concept of functional space.

In Subaekdang, five rooms have roofs, and the rest are open to the sky. Although the dining room is used as the dining room while the bathroom used as the bathroom, they can also be something else. Some of the rooms are filled with water, others filled with flowers, and some remain empty. I used white for the material surroundings of the rooms to create a sense of emptiness. I imagine the husband, a retired public official, and the wife, an artist, living an abundant life, enjoying the changes of the nature contained in the space. This house is part of the permanent collection of the Museum of Modern Art, New York.

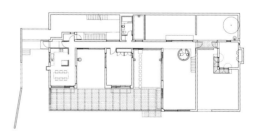

Welcomm City

Seoul

1999

The client Welcomm, the abbreviation for 'Well Communication', is a unique company in Korea. Unlike most advertisement firms in Korea which are subsidiaries within large corporations, Welcomm is an independent establishment that consistently pursues innovation and creativity. The task of the project was to design a building that reflected their creativity. It is also a building that reflects the landscape of Seoul. Seoul is a city within mountains. Old Seoul was characterized by an architectural landscape composed of small units. Against its unique topography, the last century saw Seoul filled with buildings built as if they were on the flat cities in the West. This has resulted in the disruption of the old harmony of the city. Welcomm City's neighborhood is comprised of small lots and small units. I maintain this landscape by breaking up the scale of the building. The architectural units of Seoul must remain small.

On the sloping site, a flat podium was set. A box was placed on top of the podium and three sections were cut out of the box. Through these void spaces, the neighborhood in the front and the back were connected. Through these purposeless, empty spaces, the landscape of the neighborhood became the façade. Welcomm City acts as a device for the city; it is an ethical architecture. The podium, elevated from the road, belongs to the ground. It provides for public functions with a lobby, meeting rooms, and exhibition halls. The upper levels are suited for the creative work of the firm. The boxes were clad in Corten steel, underlining the sense of passing time. The concrete ground extends to the lower podium. Because the mass was divided, the inner spaces have a dynamic connection. The stairs seem to climb up on a mountainside village. In 2000, the same year Welcomm City was completed, the theme of the Venice Biennale was 'Less Aesthetics, More Ethics'.

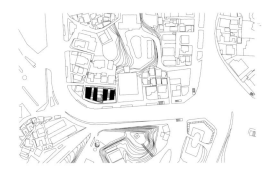

Hyehwa Culture Center
of Daejeon University

Daejeon

2001

The Daejeon University campus is situated on a steep mountain slope. With little flat ground, the mountain slope has been cut up to form flat land for building. In the existing school plan, the student center was to be placed on an embankment created by filling up a valley. With Min Hyun Sik, who was to design the dormitory down the valley, we easily came to the conclusion that the sloped topography of the site should be maintained. Hyehwa Culture Center, providing a multipurpose theatre, meeting rooms, a language center, student cafeteria, student club halls, a counseling center, and exhibition space, was to be the focal point of the university. Because of the wide range of the program, it needed spaces that allowed for different events occurring at the same time. I also did not want to constrict active students to stay indoors. I thus needed more allowance for exterior spaces.

The steep site had a 10m level difference. My first move was to set a ground plane. In order to connect this newly forged land to the road and to create a sense of place, the 3,300m² plane was lifted up like a plateau. The hilly slope, maintaining the memory of the valley, was left intact as an outdoor gathering space. Integrated into a circulation path, the facilities were arranged around this outdoor gathering space. Two glass boxes are placed on the new plateau with small meeting spaces, benches, and trees between them. It is a park, a plaza, a courtyard. Whether it is by walking up the surrounding road, through the balcony in front of the restaurant, stepping up the central courtyard, up through either of the glass boxes, or entering from the road, there are many different routes to this space. I wanted this empty area, a special space floating above the ground, to provide a place for intellectual discussions on the campus. I thus called it 'Campus Plateau'.

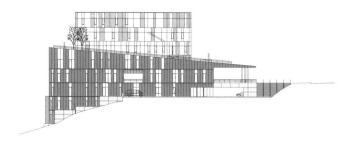

Commune by the Great Wall

Badaling, Beijing, China

2001

This project, my first built work in China is located in a beautiful valley on the boundary of the Great Wall near the outskirts of Beijing. The client's initial intention was to build 100 villas and sell them to the upper class in China. Later on, the villas were changed to hotel facilities and thus more people have come to experience the Commune. The client selected twelve architects in Asia to each design a pilot house. I was assigned to the clubhouse, a 3,300m² facility that was large in comparison to the scale of the mountainous site. I therefore divided the building into several units to work alongside nature. This building is not an object but a landscape, a place where people gather within nature—what I have come to call a 'culturescape'. The main facilities of the clubhouse—restaurants, an indoor swimming pool, a small gallery, a grocery store, and employee accommodations—were to be used by weekend residents and visitors. It was also intended to be a diplomatic club for meetings and cultural events.

There were many Yangsu trees on the site and I vowed not to cut a single tree down. The entire volume was divided like bars projecting from the northern mountain. Its occupants would climb along the topography of the bars like terraced farms. The bars are arranged so that the existing trees become part of the gardens. Some trees even penetrated the building. Decks and water ponds at the boundary of the bars were designed to float out into the existing topography, manifesting the original shape of the land. In plan, the interior and exterior of the building are almost indistinguishable. I was able to maintain the idea of the sketch I drew at the first site visit because of the strong initial impression of the land. Even before its completion, the project became world renown and the client became the first non-architect to receive special recognition at the Venice Biennale.

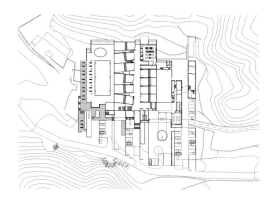

Paju Bookcity

Paju, Gyeonggi-do

1999

In the early 1990's, a group of leading publishers sought a new cultural vision of Korean society through a radical relocation of the publishing industry. It was through their initiative that the 990,000m² Paju Bookcity was born. As the architectural coordinator of this new city, I moved against the conventional master plan that had already obtained government approval, and convinced the publisher's union of a new approach to the urban design and architecture of the city. Collaborating with Florian Beigel, Min Hyun Sik, Kim Jong Kyu, and Kim Young Joon, we redesigned the master plan. Following Beigel's idea for a 'Landscape Script', we established a consistent set of architectural principles according to the distinct nature of the different areas on the site: the highway shadow type alongside the main highway, the bookshelf type in the center, the stone type in the wetlands, the canal loft type by the stream, and the urban island type by the access roads. After the master plan was established, 40 Korean and international architects were invited to design the individual lots. Only a few lots strayed from the guidelines. Most of them worked after a common understanding of the spirit of this city. However, with the road plans fixed by the government master plan, there was a harsh limit to what we could do.

As the architectural coordinator, I supervised the direction of all the projects and designed the infrastructure of this city—such as roadside facilities, street lights, bridges, temporary restaurants, and memorial installations—so as to maintain its identity. By the end of the 2000's, overcoming much difficulty, the construction of the first phase was nearing completion. A city, however, is never complete because it is a living organism. As its second phase moves on, Paju Bookcity will continue to grow and change.

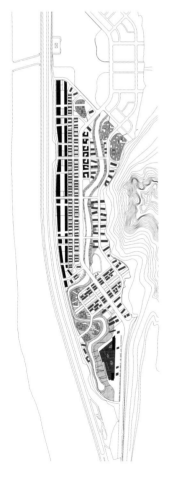

Korea National University of Arts
Master Plan

Seoul
2000

This is a project that was only partially realized. With public officials arbitrarily manipulating the planning process, I was only marginally involved in the implementation of the master plan. I do not usually look back at a failed project; however, I had the precious experience of expanding the boundary of architecture from establishment of space to the management of a city with this plan. The site of the new campus is located next to the royal tomb of the 20th king of the Joseon Dynasty. Backed by a mountain and facing water, it has the typical topography of a propitious site. During the latter half of the 20th century, it was occupied by the Korean Central Intelligence Agency (KCIA). It was a blank space on the map. The dormitory, shooting range, and garages of the KCIA, de facto illegal according to the Cultural Properties Protection Law, damaged the landscape. My master plan sought to recover the original ground to create what I call the 'culturescape'.

According to the original shape of the site, the position of the buildings were set to form three basic levels: one, the original ground level; two, the floating artificial ground which centralized the activities of the new campus; and three, an integrated building level that metaphorically restored the damaged land. The facilities providing for all cultural and artistic events were focused on the deck. The buildings were composed like a maze that supported unexpected creative activities. A campus spine integrates the entire site, managing and mediating the scattered facilities. This new axis, set in the same direction of the stream, is linked to many small roads. No one knows what will happen in these spaces. This anticipation of the unknown is essential to the arts. I believe it is the basis for the identity and continuity of our existence.

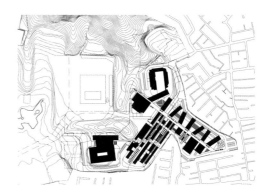

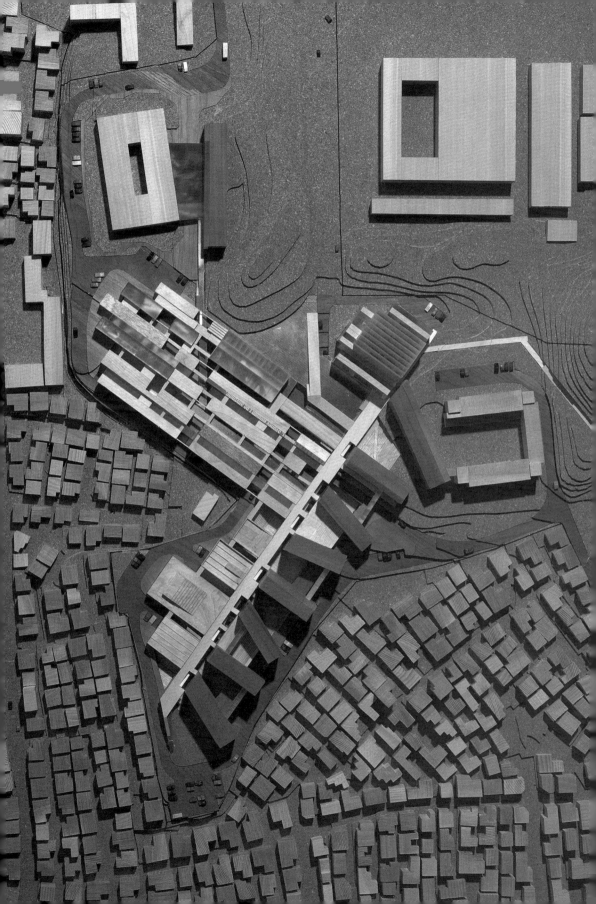

Boao Canal Village

Hainan Province, China

2001

Boao is a small village located on the east coast of Hainan Island in China. Hainan Island is a resort destination with a subtropical climate, a population of 8 million, and a size of 34,000m². SOHO China, a developer based in Beijing, planned this resort village of 400 villas. In July 2002, the company requested a master plan to be designed within one month, stating that it would be first used as lodging for the 2003 Boao Forum for Asia. It was a hurried schedule. The land was beautiful, a primitive forest without any infrastructure. Ventilation and shading was a requirement because the humidity was so high.

Due to flooding concerns during the rainy season, the road and the floor of the houses were raised above the ground. This architectural style, commonly used in tropical buildings, was also necessary to preserve the vulnerable ecosystem of the land. I wanted to resort to the idea that building is merely a temporary borrowing of the land. There were two basic housings types: the water-front type and forest-front type. Both types receive and circulate wind, the interior left open as one room. The long void between the houses also plays the same role. Wind speed will change as it passes through these shaded spaces. Before the construction drawings were complete, the client began selling the land. Amazingly, the next year, Boao Forum for Asia was hosted here. The village was built in 8 months. It was a miracle.

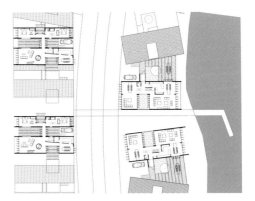

Reed House

Yangpyeong, Gyeonggi-do

2002

Reed House was designed for the president of Welcomm. While the Welcomm headquarters were under construction, the client was living next to the eventual site of this house. There was a development boom in the area and the client became worried about the unsightly encroachments to come. He first purchased additional land to create a birch tree forest, and then the Reed House lot, on which there were two existing houses of heavy dark red bricks surrounded by a spacious green lawn. He thus came to possess a large amount of land and planned to build several guest houses. Because of our similar architectural preferences, we easily came to agree on the form of the new houses. Replacing the western lawn with silver sawgrass and creating a birch tree forest, we decided to locate the houses inside the forest. The long hours of discussions with the client were focused not on the house itself but on how to compose the land.

Considering the size of the 200m long site, I drew a wooden box 4.8m by 36m. Because flood water levels rise up to 2 to 3m above ground level, the main floor is located on the upper level and work rooms and storage on the ground level. The outhouse was placed in front of the main house to take advantage of the view from inside the house to the outside scenery. The silver horizontal roof finished with titanium finds harmony with the thick birch tree forest. Only from the opposite side of the river can the entire house with the silver horizontal roof be seen. I did not design a house to be seen, but a house to see the landscape.

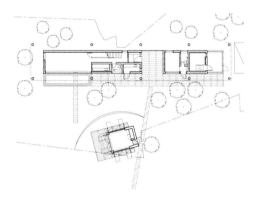

Dr. Park Gallery

Yangpyeong, Gyeonggi-do
2003

As I was finishing the design of the Reed House along Namhan River, I received a project for an art gallery and residence on the other side of the river. I naively thought that if these two projects were completed, the self-indulgent amusement park landscape of the riverside would succumb to the river's more natural forces.

The long and narrow site lies between a highway and the river exposed to the vehicular traffic. Located on the curve of a road, the building appears suddenly to the passing cars. A design method was required to reduce the speed so that its architecture could be embraced. River and road regulations disallowed a building to go beyond 6m in width. A single building spanning the entire site would interfere with the view of the river. The river should look more beautiful with the presence of the architecture. For these reasons, the entire mass was divided into two parts: the house and the art gallery. The gallery was again divided into smaller masses to allow the in-between voids to mediate the river and the road. These segmented masses were combined to create a series of landscape spaces. The long parallel view flows in the direction of the river with irregular cross sections. The unaligned masses, the spaces in-between, and the long flow of the river slow down the speed of the passing cars. These masses were clad in Corten steel. The green mountains and water behind the dark red mass are beautiful. The acute angles of the rusted steel masses may come from a personal obsession that weight has to be secured in this era of intolerable lightness. When viewed from the opposite side of the river, the buildings are inevitably back-lighted by the sun. I emphasized the feeling of mass rather than of architecture so that the land may be more clearly recognized. However, with the commercialism of the area swarming over like a monsoon, I realized the futility of my own desperate ambitions.

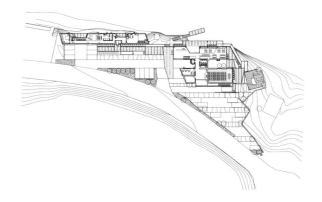

Lock Museum

Seoul

2002

The Lock Museum is located in the Dongsung-dong neighborhood. Dongsung means east of Sunggyobang, an old Joseon Dynasty area where Confucianism was taught. In the latter half of the 20th century, it was the site of the main campus of Seoul National University, until it moved out in 1975, when the entire campus was sold as residential plots. As the headquarters and cultural facilities of the Arts Council Korea were established around the Maronie Park, there was hope that a cultural village would be formed. However, with the rapid commercialization of the area, land prices soared and the neighborhood became an entertainment district, forcing small galleries and bookstores to leave. Buildings imitating Mexican styles or Disney castles sprang up. The city lost its ethics. The site was located on the street at the back of the Maronie Park, which continues to provide a gap of fresh air. Placed just outside the original Seoul National University campus, it is the starting point of a neighborhood of simple houses that climb up the slope of Naksan Mountain.

The client, a master craftsman who manufactures high-quality architectural metal hardware, is a collector of locks and metalware. He wanted a museum of his collection within a building that also included his own house, space for cultural events, and a restaurant and design shop that would generate income to help maintain the building. This crowded neighborhood of infinite eclectic styles, disordered signboards, cluttered power lines and utility poles needed a place of weight. The weight of the project lies in its simplicity. This building without windows or decoration confronted its surroundings with the weight of its steel. Its negative emptiness creates a tension within a landscape of enmity. The interior, on the other hand, is clear and bright.

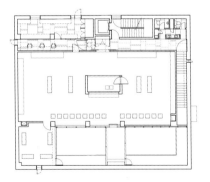

Humax Village

Seongnam, Gyeonggi-do

2002

As a first-generation venture company, Humax, is led by innovators who enjoy the challenges of the future. Rejecting the existing outdated office, they wanted a new kind of working space. The interface with the city provided the clue for their new office. Located along the boundary of the satellite town of Bundang, the spine of the site curves at the center and faces the river. The high-rise boxes of this area are isolated from these surroundings. As one of the last empty lots of the area, this site was an oasis. A transparent architecture was a necessary as a bridge between the urban landscape and the surrounding nature. Another reason for this building's transparency was the open community that Humax sought.

Its collectivity begins on the inside. In the center of the inner space, a big deep floor, a courtyard is opened to the sky. Penetrating through thirteen vertically connected floors, this space sustains a different spatial structure for each level. The stairs are like Jacob's ladder and the elevators are time machines. This place can be an interior or an exterior as well as a small park or small plaza. The plaza is the most important element in the identity of Humax's community. Just as the exterior embodies the interior, the inside is structured like a city. There are plazas, main roads, side streets, and dead ends. There is also an interior park with trees and grass. It rains and snows inside and sunlight penetrates deep down.

Humax is not just a building, but a community village. Not only due to its large scale, populated by 2,000 people, but also for the office life acts as a temporary society, it remains a beautiful memory for the youth. Thus, I named this building 'Humax Village'.

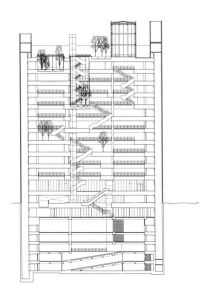

Chaowai SOHO

Beijing, China

2005

In the early 2000's, as a project to develop central Beijing into a modern city, Beijing pursued an ambitious plan, called CBD, centered on Changan Grand Street, as it intersected the three ring roads of the city. Chaowai SOHO is located in the north-western corner of the Beijing CBD. The developer SOHO China gave just two weeks of preparation for the competition. The 20,000m² site was located in an area originally outside the Beijing castle gate, which may have been used as farmland or periphery functions during older times. More recently, the area had been mostly vacant with a few public buildings. The CBD master plan projected a central green axis penetrating the city center. For this project, connecting the green axis to the crossing point next to the site had the highest priority. I therefore created a plaza at the center of the site and called it the Bazaar. From this central plaza, I set off small streets as a metaphor of the alleyways of the *hutong*, placing shops that would connect to the city roads.

In creating a community within this large mass, the entire site was enclosed with a massive band of studio-type offices that I perceived as kind of *tulou*, an earthwork wall. On the rooftop of the lower levels of the earthwork, a park was created for rest and festive occasions. The office space that was taken out for these public spaces was compensated by adding height to the central office tower that looked over the community like a watchtower. As a result, there is an abundance of plazas, courtyards, parks, and streets shared by all. The interior is full of life and diversity as a city should be. I call this project Small Beijing. I did the competition design in a very short period of time, like a passing storm. I won the competition and this small city inside Beijing was realized.

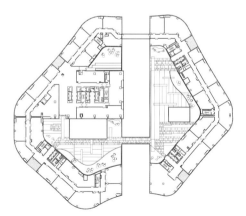

Cheonan Oriental Hospital
of Daejeon University

Cheonan, Chungcheongnam-do

2003

Cheonan Oriental Hospital is a specialized hospital for oriental treatment and healing. Considerations for the elderly, long-stay patients, and the disabled are important, and the hospital thus require a different space than western medicine based hospitals. Because many of their patients stay for an extended period of time, the hospital rooms become a community space. Therefore, unlike the typical linear formation of patient rooms, this hospital required spaces for sharing. I provided courtyards to promote the community spirit, roads on which to walk and stroll, and green for rest and the enjoyment of watching the sunset. This hospital is located on the outskirts of the booming city of Cheonan, in a neighborhood experiencing rapid urban development. Across the hospital lies a mountain, albeit deformed by civil works that functions as bulwark against the flood of commercial development. The rush of traffic, flashy commercial signboards, motels, and bars threaten the tranquility required of a hospital. In order to maintain a stable atmosphere, I created multiple layers of space to protect the hospital. The spaces between the partitions are allotted as public area, often forming semi-exterior spaces. The terraces have open views to the green mountain, part of a pleasant park environment for patients who stroll around the hospital. I used basalt rock for the exterior cladding for its natural texture and color and its affinity to Oriental medicine. The rhythm of the irregular window pattern and gap between the basal rock panels emulate the speed of the adjacent highways.

DMZ Peace and Life Valley

Inje, Gangwon-do

2006

DMZ Peace and Life Valley is an organization that promotes 'Opening Peace with the Key of Life'. With the full support of Gangwon-do, it is comprised of activists and intellectuals who are working to restore the ecological life of the DMZ, the Demilitarized Zone. In an era of confrontation, it pursues the dignity of life by healing the wounds of war. It serves primarily as the base camp for the survey of the DMZ but also provides programs for lectures, seminars, meditation, and agricultural activities.

Placed on a hill close to the DMZ at the border of Inje district, the facility seeks a close relationship with nature. The hill forms a central basin open to the west. In a virgin site empty of building, the first architectural intervention must function as a medium. Between the road, a symbol of modern civilization, and nature, an artificial nature and a naturalized artifice seemed right. The site has a 25m height difference. The main facilities were placed on the flat basin area in the middle. Looking from the road, it looks like a village of buildings, yards, and pathways. When climbing through the empty gaps between the buildings, the structure disappears and just the scene of nature remains. One side of the building is clad in Corten steel, holding memory, and the other side is an earthen wall. The land and the building become one body. It is an architecture of the ground and an architecture of landscape.

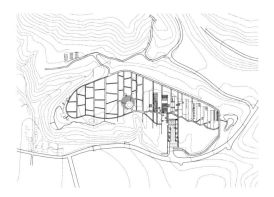

Guduk Presbyterian Church

Busan

2006

Originated from the Latin *ecclesia*, a 'church' designates the meeting of the called people. Thus, the word does not solely define the building. There is no given form of the church. Jesus preached the gospel on the Galilean beaches and the mountains outside Jerusalem. These gatherings can be said to provide the true model of the church. The first goal of building a church is to secure piety; that is, to create a separation from the world. It should impress on the people, not God. In Christianity, God is an omnipresent being that does not just exist in the church. Believing that God is present inside the church and adorning it like a shrine violates the spirit of Christianity. A person is born with original sin but is saved by the death of Jesus. Man is always captured by temptations as a living being. With the power of the Holy Spirit, the constant examining and cultivating of oneself to live rightfully constitutes the religious life of a Christian. A building that only provides for worship and ceremony at a set time does not constitute the true nature of the church. The most important moment in religious life is when someone seeks the grace of God. The church does not have a special form. When the Christians themselves are ecclesial, bound to the being of God, the space they occupy becomes a church. Are the 60,000 churches in this country ecclesial? I doubt it.

The Guduk Presbyterian Church is special to me. I was born and raised as a member of this church. Though I moved to Seoul to go to college, the memory of this church provided a strong foundation for my life. The road up to the church, the surrounding alley and yard, the fig tree, the wooden floor, and the bell tower are alive in my memory, always comforting me. 40 years after I left, this project was built on the pieces of these memories.

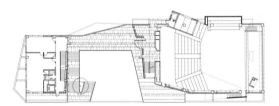

Traditional Buddhism
Culture Center of Jogye Order

Gongju, Chungcheongnam-do

2007

Records of Buddhist architecture are nearly nonexistent in Korea because during the 600 years of the Joseon Dynasty, Buddhism had been suppressed by Confucianism. That is why today Buddhism is obsessed with keeping to old principles. Such an attitude goes against the populace and contemporaneity, and thus against the very principles of Buddhism. Whether I would be selected as the architect of this project was a decisive moment. After much contemplation, the leaders of the Jogye Order chose the progressive path and accepted my architecture. I gained much wisdom about architecture from the emptiness of Buddhist architecture. The principle of Buddhist architecture, as of Buddhism itself, is emptiness. Therefore, despite anything, emptiness had to be the essence of this building.

The site, 1km apart along the creek from Magoksa Temple, is formed as basin by the curving stream. One Buddhist monk told me that the land was shaped like an ark. The site contained a Joseon Dynasty rooftile kiln, and thus many parts of the site were prohibited from building. The clients thought this was an unfortunate condition, but I felt the opposite. It allowed the central area of the site to remain empty. The courtyards, positioned here and there, had their own mode of existence. Independent, but at times connected to each other, they contained the beauty of the surrounding landscape and traces of life. The role of the architecture was merely to set boundaries. Though the facilities were scattered along the entire site, there was a loose axis connecting them. The axis extended into the void between the valleys, a view of empty space. The building materials are wood, stone, and earth. They will all eventually meld into the ground and disappear. The only thing remaining will be emptiness.

Chusa Memorial Museum

Jeju-do

2008

If Koreans did not have Jeju Island, our outlook on the horizon would have been very confined. With beautiful volcanic cones, hummocks, the transparent sea, dark basalt rocks, and lustrous vegetation, Jeju has made us yearn for a nirvana. Though it now bustles with Chinese tourists, a sad history is engraved into its beautiful landscape. Deep wounds remain from foreign invasion by Mongols and the Japanese. It was constantly exploited by the main land. Ideological conflicts of the 20th century brought tragic consequences that still scar the present. Furthermore, as the toughest place of exile, its culture is deeply engraved by the sorrows of the persecuted. Kim Jeong Hee (1786-1856), known by his sobriquet Chusa, was the most famous of such exiles. Chusa, the finest intellect of the late Joseon Dynasty, reached his highest artistic stage during the eight years of exiled solitude in Jeju. His writing and calligraphy, which look like they have been picked with awls, were the product of this solitude.

An architecture that commemorates Chusa must free itself of all frivolous desire. The site lies next to an old fortress. Within the fortress, a village of small, simple houses forms a luscious landscape. A 1,200m² building is a large structure for this area. The priority was to build an invisible building. Hence, most of the volume was placed underground with the smallest and the simplest building above-ground. The sunken yard provides for sunlight and ventilation. When finishing the tour of the museum, you come to the open space above ground. After climbing the steps, one faces Chusa in empty silence.

Anticipating a grandiose building, the locals were disappointed by this common-looking wooden building with a gable roof. I heard that they mocked the building calling it a potato depot. I told them that this made me happy. A memorial to Chusa had to be a potato depot.

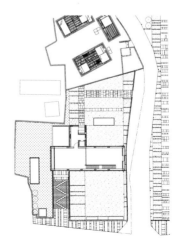

Daejanggol New Town
Master Plan

Hwaseong, Gyeonggi-do
2006

Rebuking Le Corbusier's idea for the new city of the 20th century, Henri Lefebvre wrote: "In such a thoroughly programmed machine for living, there is no adventure or romance, and it divides and blocks us all to depart from each other". He lamented the extinction of regional identity; different lands and different lives forced into a standard model and a monotonous landscape. According to François Ascher's concept of 'Metapolis', against the idea of the ever-expanding 'Metropolis', a modern city community should be composed of multiple, complex, and independent spaces of real life. Looseness, uncertainty, union and solidarity, eco-system and environment, creation and change are the key concepts of the 'Metapolis'.

Daejanggol New Town targeted creative professionals working in small units, totaling 10,000 people and 3,000 housing units. Daejanggol sought to merge the country and the city, to foster the coexistence of the old and young generations. The 992,000m² site, only 15km south of Seoul, previously contained 50 houses scattered along several smaller valleys. A diverse landscape flowed along the gradual incline of the valleys. From the topography, the town takes on a branch pattern like fingers, inter-connecting town and nature. Respecting the pre-existing spatial structure, water flow, and ridge lines, the urban structure is comprised of vegetation (green network), water systems (blue network), vehicles (red network), bicycles (silver network), and pedestrian systems (yellow network). At every node of these intertwining lines, meeting places, bicycle parking, stores, galleries, and bookstores were located as small footholds for the town's cultural activities. This kind of project for an emerging community was a way to reform society. However, information about the project was leaked to speculators, putting an end to the project.

In collaboration with Min Hyun Sik, Yi Jongho, Kim Young Joon

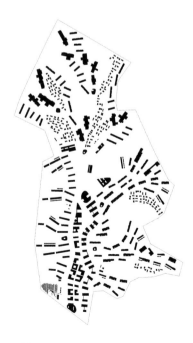

Qianmendajie Historical Area Preservation and Regeneration Plan

Beijing, China

2008

The axis of the Forbidden City is not only the physical axis of the city but also the psychological and symbolic axis of the Chinese people and the nation. Placed on this axis, Qianmendajie refers to the 'road of the emperor', the stepping way to the ancestral rites of the Temple of Heaven. This axis now extends to the Olympic Park north of the Forbidden City. The Qianmendajie is a record of Beijing. As the foothold for the entrance to the Forbidden City, dispatched regional officers and students found residence while maintaining their traditional culture. Both building traditions unique to Beijing and those of the provinces are discovered in the area. The eastern sector, which includes the 800m long main street, was the 230,000m^2 project site. The area is comprised of *siheyuan*, the traditional Chinese house, albeit transformed under the communist regime. Large portions were destroyed and replaced by western style buildings. The older residents had already been evicted and the site was a ruin. Because of its political and symbolic importance, the area is under a strict city planning regulation.

The area is a unique amalgam of spaces. The alleyways are deep and slender, seemingly all connected but then suddenly blocked. The area is both a documentary and a drama on spatial wisdom. Its traces were like a strong landscript. I divided the entire structure into four city types: the labyrinth type, constituted by the transformed spatial structure of *siheyuan*; the bar-code type, adapted spaces for new programs; the precinct type, consisting of restored traditional housing; and the urban mass type located near Qianmendajie. Thus, the new plan looked very familiar. Overlapping it with the original map of the area demonstrated that much of the existing spatial structure was preserved. For the old buildings that were destroyed, the pattern of the space was engraved on the ground. It was a configuration drawn, not on a blank paper, but on an old palimpsest. It was a result of adding my ideas on to an already-written text. A spatial abundance, impossible from the hand of one person, was created.

However, after the Beijing Olympics marathon passed through Qianmendajie, this project was given to others. In the end, I was excluded from the project, resulting in a wholly different approach. The redevelopment of the area was so urgent that they filled it with building reproductions from the era of the old Republic of China.

Kyobo Paju Center

Paju, Gyeonggi-do
2007

As one of the last buildings of the first phase of Paju Bookcity, the project followed its design guidelines and adjusted to the arrangement of the existing buildings. The linear green belt crossing the entire complex divided the lot into two parts. As a 'bookshelf type' specified in the design guidelines, it provided visual corridors for the residents in the buildings, both in the front and the rear. It required segmentation. This strict condition was employed to make this complex a unity. The building was again segmented by connecting the visual paths created by the small lots across the 10m road. It was one building made out of seven boxes, whose size, floor height, and form were adjusted to become part of the rhythm of the street. Functionally, the lower levels required one flat space, which was set as a podium and was finished with glass to reduce the heavy feeling of the basalt mass placed on top. The view of the Han River and Simhaksan Mountain grace its entrance. The essence of Kyobo Paju Center is that it is the realization of good intentions, an agreement to form a commonality in Paju Bookcity.

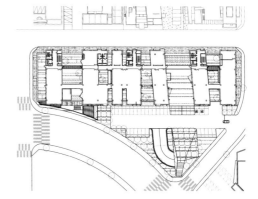

30th Anniversary Memorial Building of Daejeon University

Daejeon

2008

This project was the climax of the comprehensive campus plan for Daejeon University, ambitiously pursued as part of its 30th anniversary. The site, located at the rear of the central library, is the place that forms a strong axis from the west gate, and is connected to the pedestrian-only road toward the south gate. It is a central area that brings the campus spine to penetrate the entire campus. The mountain to the south, though covered with trees, had been devastated by civil works and needed repair. The master plan required a symbolic twin tower, which I was completely against. It was not the type of architecture that this land needed. Towers that dominate their surroundings went against the essence of the university; that is, the pursuit of a free democratic society.

I wanted to recover the topography through architecture. I analyzed the program, formed several units, and arranged them according to the original topography. Following the master plan, I brought in the sloped road, starting from the west gate plaza, into the building and created a valley pathway. This valley is the busiest part of the building. By connecting the two divided parts from top to bottom, it created a flexible scene. The rooftop of the building becomes a new ground, continuously connected to the deep yards between the segmented masses. Here and there round and rectangular volumes occupy the rooftops to inspire both curiosity and suspicion. The shape of the building is of course not important here. The more important thing is that it should be a place that activates potential and generates action. It is impossible to predict exactly which will occur here. However, as long as the university society encourages and protects intellect, we can remain optimistic. I indulged in the establishment of places and sites that were without a set program. It was an architecture created through assemblage.

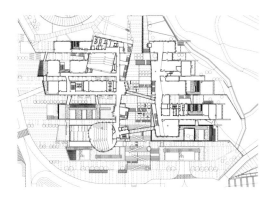

Jemunheon

Gwangju

2010

Located at the boundary of the Gwangju Biennale and Yongbongje, the lake park, Jemunheon functions as the support center for the Biennale. One may expect that the neighborhood of a biennale would have a cultural atmosphere, but that is not the case in Gwangju. High-rise apartment complexes and disorderly shops, typical in the outskirts of provincial Korean cities, surround the biennale area. The goal of the project was to preserve the cultural landscape of the biennale through a new architectural intervention. The plaza between this building and the biennale exhibition hall is an important space for visitors and artists, a key site for the memory of the biennale. However, the existing plaza is a barren space, simultaneously rough and frivolous. To function as a firm background to the plaza, a strong wall was built to limit and protect it. The two spaces of the Gwangju Biennale and Yongbongje become equivalent to a relationship between the city and nature. The wall both divides and connects. The wall facing west blocks the late afternoon sun even as its brown concrete surface reflects the sunlight.

Within these walls lies a small complex: a small courtyard, a park, a corridor for people to meet. I changed the boundary of the space by inserting a black box into the middle layer of the brown wall at a skewed angle. This angled box was directed towards the entrance road, securing a natural access to the surroundings. It also enabled nearby residents to cross into the outdoor theatre to enjoy the landscape. Jemunheon supports an international culture but also provides for the daily lives of the neighborhood.

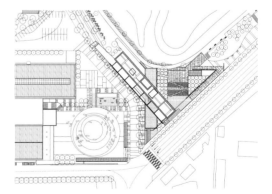

Moheon

Moheon is an extension of a house that the client had lived in for 40 years. It consists of a guest bedroom, a *sarangchae* (main quarter), a small inner garden, and a larger garden. The challenge was to create a rich space from a small floor area. The 330m² site was divided into four yards. To maximize the front yard, the inner space was set back and divided by a linear garden. The front dining area was made transparent so that the garden could be seen from the bedroom. One side of the yard was filled with water, and the other was lowered to allow light to enter into the basement. From the outside window of the bedroom, which can be seen from the connecting path, a thick bamboo yard created a rich multi-layered space comprised of the front garden, dining room, the in-between garden, bedroom, and back yard. The transparent dining space with the variable wooden-panel wall enlarged the sense of scale of the lot. The entire lot was surrounded by a Corten steel wall, maximizing the tension of the surrounding space.

The landscaping by Chong Youngsun surpassed anything I could have ever imagined. She maximized a space that was only 165m² and 9m deep. I imagined a few thick white-stem trees in a black Corten steel background. But Chong created a primitive forest: a small dense grove of wild pear trees with the ground filled with small, rough stones. Seemingly insignificant pear trees fill the garden with their brilliant red. The building disappears in the landscape.

Seated on the *hanok* (Korean traditional house) guest room floor, opening the *deulchang* (swinging window) looking over the water garden, seeing through the transparent dining space, we are presented with this deep, dark landscape. I call the house Moheon, a 'House for Anyone'. The building has abandoned itself. It is a demonstration of the beauty of absence.

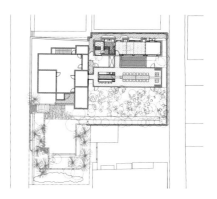

Graveyard for President
Roh Moo-hyun

Gimhae, Gyeongsangnam-do

2009

Roh Moo-hyun, the former President of Korea, was a person who always kept himself outside the boundaries. His life before his presidency was this way, as were his last moments. He explicitly stated that he would not be buried at the National Cemetery. The conventional rituals of burial were certainly inadequate for him. If the tomb is for the deceased, the graveyard is more a space for the living to visit and to reflect. There was no other style more fitting for President Roh's burial grounds than the Jongmyo Shrine podium, a place left empty so the living may call on the dead.

At the edge of Roh Moo-hyun's hometown of Bongha Village, under Bonghwasan Mountain, there was a triangular-shaped field. A place where the Owl Rock stands, this land of about 3,300m^2 sat right next to two traversing streams. These streams divided the land into three parts, making it right for an ancestral site to be divided into an entrance, main ritual area, and the grave. Located at the intersection of the village and the mountain, it was a terminus for outside visitors. To address concerns of flooding, the entire ground was raised 1.5m. Raising the land is a process of lifting a space out of the everyday. A triangular pond was placed at the vertex of the entrance so visitors can wash their minds. Past this and up the stairs, the entire expanse of the plateau is covered with rough stone plates that ever-slightly slope up and down. The lines dividing the stone plates that cover the floor are comprised of smooth blocks of inscribed stones. This is a landscript. 15,000 epitaphs written by ordinary citizens are engraved onto the stones. The president's grave is covered by a large flat rock. A 60m Corten steel wall, modeled after the walls surrounding the royal tombs, forms the boundary between the mountain and the platform. Most visitors linger after paying their respects. As they walk around this unfamiliar village, they read the writings on the stone plates, cross the streams, and tread on the rough surfaces. Maybe it is a way of comforting themselves, thinking about themselves. Though the writing on the stone will eventually disappear under their footsteps, the memory will forever remain. That is why this burial ground is called 'Landscape for the Self-Deported People'.

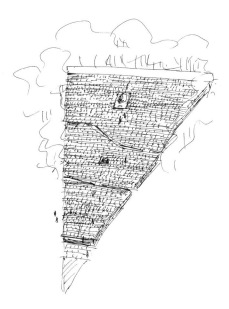

Shin Dongyeop
Literary Museum

Buyeo, Chungcheongnam-do

2009

"Who claims to have seen the sky? / Without a single blossom of cloud, / who claims to have seen the sky? "
The literary museum of the poet Shin Dongyeop (1930-1969), the author who penned these lines, is located in his hometown Buyeo, next to the house where he had lived. The house was a small cottage that had long remained in disarray, in a way similar to the poet's own life of grief endured during a time of disharmony. The house commemorating this poet, who cried out toward our unhappy era 'Go away, the shells!', is both less and more a commemoration. Wouldn't it be more correct to commemorate ourselves and the land we are standing on through the poet? I wanted a path through the museum, ultimately returning to the beginning, to be a way of finding ourselves, a way of embracing the poet Shin Dongyeop in all of us.

Thus, the house has a circular path. Passing the house where the poet lived and entering the museum through the *madang*, visitors are guided to the central courtyard, and as one walks up these comfortable steps of the courtyard, a new ground appears. This ground is then connected to another level, and then to another level. As one circles, and the level gets lower, the path returns to the ground of everyday life. Visitors arrive to a plaza with waving flags containing the words of the poet, a work created by the artist Lim Ok Sang. Here, beautiful words are scattered in the air. As visitors delve into the fragments, they return to the starting point without knowing it.

This architecture is the medium in creating this process—form should be absent. It is an architecture of rough concrete that does not commemorate itself. It is the proper way to respect a poet who denounced the shells.

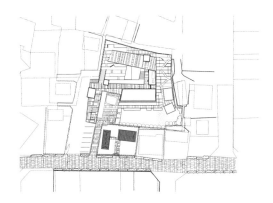

Earth, Water, Flower, Wind
360° Golf Clubhouse

Yeoju, Gyeonggi-do

2009

Earth, Water, Flower, Wind. The special name of this golf course is a symbol for nature. It means that nature is that which recharges the energy exhausted by everyday urban life. The clubhouse then, serves as the gateway on the path from the city to nature and the medium in which daily life becomes extraordinary. So, as the two different sectors intermix, a dramatic shift occurs in the space. Moreover, with so many people who don't know each other gathered together at the same time, this place takes on the characteristics of a village.

The clubhouse was built in the shape of several houses gathered together. It carries out the operational requirements of a system that sometimes needs to move rapidly. That is, after setting each volume that is suitable for each individual function unit, they are connected as an irregular group in the most intimate manner. The spaces between the individual units become courtyards that provide natural ventilation and sunlight and a visually abundant spatial feeling. The volumes are composed of one or two floors, reinforcing the idea of a house with a gable roof. The shape of the roofed ensemble resembles a small village or mountain temple. The exterior wall finish is composed of concrete and stone. It creates a background that adapts to the beautiful changes in nature. It boasts wooden projections in the openings that soften its rough properties. Guests look at this clubhouse from various points in the field. When they stand on the last hole, the scenery bathed in the light reflected by the titanium roofs constitutes the finale. For those who finish all the courses and return to their daily lives, 'Earth, Water, Flower, Wind' become more than words and a memory of the space.

Office Building of
Samyang Chemical Company

Seoul

2013

In the history of building technology, Rome's invention of concrete was a revolutionary event. It changed a natural tradition of building materials that had continued for several thousands of years. Later in the Gothic era, building technology achieved another high technological achievement. Creative structures such as columns, buttresses, and flying girders were made to support the roof, allowing the construction of tall buildings and freeing walls from the burden of supporting the roof. Perhaps, Le Corbusier's domino frame was a modern rearrangement of this Gothic technology. It was the basis for modern office buildings, employing the curtain-like walls as partitions dividing the inside from outside.

Against this principle, I decided to create a different solution for the Office Building of Samyang Chemical Company. That is, by returning to the traditional structural use and function of the wall, the curtain walls were removed. By doing so, the space within the walls took on the role of the columns, creating a free plan and lowering energy use. Most of all, the office recovers a spatial sense of the tectonic, lost in the free plan.

The district plan specified a park to the north. Following this plan, an interior space open towards the north, as an extension of the park, was created. Thereafter, the core and corridors were formed. With the shared atrium space as the center, the movements inside and out are exposed to each other. I believe that an urban community can be developed in this space. Unfortunately, due to changes in the interior, the strength of the space has been weakened. However, as long as the firm concrete structural wall establishes the space, that strength will always exist. It is the basis of the genuine spirit of the building.

Toechon House

Gwangju, Gyeonggi-do

2009

Toechon means 'village of those who have retreated from official service'. This 165m² house was designed for a professor of economics and his wife, a humanities professor. The husband, a progressive academic, commissioned the house so that he and his wife could stay next to his mother and live with their son, a student of jazz piano. As academics, they needed independent studies while the son needed a separate room for the piano. As such, the family's lifestyle provided the decisive clue for the configuration of the house. The house, while providing independent spaces for each person, brings them together to form a home. Hence, one newspaper titled its article on the house 'Separated House'. Furthermore, farmhouse laws in this area required the house to be separated into a 100m² main house and a 65m² subsidiary house. The more fundamental reason came from the traditional Korean idea of a house as a group of rooms. From one unit to ninety-nine units, the house is construed as a group of rooms. These purposeless, unspecified rooms set themselves apart by taking on independent personalities. They demonstrate that our ancestors already understood the concepts of modern architecture and implemented them in actual life. These different types of rooms all have direct access to nature, allowing abundant natural ventilation and sunlight.

They create a very healthy house. For those used to living in a closed, artificial environment, this house may feel inconvenient. But in the beautiful neighborhood of Toechon, if you are able to grow accustomed to such inconveniences, this kind of life will become irrevocably enjoyable. Have we forgotten this 'inconvenient joy'? Toechon House is a new house that carries an old memory. In this era of fragmentation, it is our old future that has to be reclaimed.

Lotte Art Villas

Jeju-do

2011

More than any contemporary map, Kim Jeongho's 19th century map *Daedongyeojido* illustrates the principle of Jeju's landscape. This map shows the ridges that stretch out from Hallasan Mountain and the valleys that extend out towards the sea. It is a vertical understanding of Jeju's topography. That is, the line of the slope connecting Hallasan Mountain and the sea is the axis of the Island's ecosystem and the flow of the landscape. This vertical axis is blocked by the 516 road that wraps around Jeju. The recently completed coast road is an anti-ecological civil construction project that transformed Jeju from an island floating on the sea to a land floating on asphalt. The buildings are the same. Arranging the buildings in a horizontal line to command the ocean view blocks the flow of the eco system and violates the public realm. We must empty the path leading from Hallasan Mountain to the sea.

The density set by the master plan was closer to that of an urban city than that of a resort town. Thus emptying the ecological path was even more essential. Block A, located at the highest point of the site, could only be made using long vertical planes because it was necessary to have large gaps between the buildings so as not to interfere with the view of Hallasan Mountain and the sea. One housing unit was set as an open one-room unit in order to keep the flow connected.

The clubhouse located at the entrance of the complex was designed with even more of an emphasis on the eco-path. Touching the ground at different levels in all directions, these levels were organically connected throughout the building. The ground suddenly becomes the rooftop terrace, and as you follow the free sloped entrance road, you arrive at another ground, and soon you are connected to the restaurant, courtyard, and gallery. It was the topography that designed these buildings.

Dormitory of CHA University

Pocheon, Gyeonggi-do

2011

The CHA University campus is located on an isolated mountain. The university took over an existing college preparatory school and used the site as its campus. As the existing buildings were finished with red brick, the new buildings used the same material. With only a few accessible facilities nearby, for the students living on campus, the dormitory is like a Buddhist temple, a monastery disconnected from the world. Of course, more open and free buildings could be installed to improve the environment, but it doesn't seem much of a consolation. I thought that creating a monastery type spatial structure would, in fact, correspond to the purpose of the dormitory. The students will not spend their entire college life here and their living environment as college students would be something special.

The site is on a relatively steep slope located behind the library at the north end of the campus. The dormitory had to be divided into several buildings. The small courtyards between the buildings, enclosed by high walls, became quiet, but powerful spaces. This spatial tension becomes an important building element and perhaps helps create a stronger sense of unity in the community. After all, didn't these students, by living in the dormitory, separate themselves from the outer world? Meticulous details and the diligent use of the material create a particular domestic landscape. With the monastery as the underlying structure, perhaps its spirit may also dwell here in this living space.

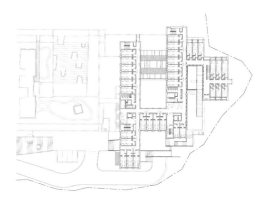

Pingdu Housing Culture Center

Pingdu, China

2012

Pingdu, with a population of 1.5 million, is a small city for China, but one that boasts 3,000 years of history. Influenced by the Qingdao region's rapid development, the city has also experienced immense change. When the public office buildings that occupied the city center moved to the newly developed area, the region underwent re-development. The new apartments and office buildings destroyed all remnants of the city's past. However, an ancient map, obtained with great difficulty, confirmed that many of the old roads still existed and were still in use. Based on the landscript of these roads, I prepared a master plan called the Pingdu Historical Area Regeneration Plan.

China Vanke, the developer of the entire project, asked me to design its public relations and cultural center on a site with a thick group of old trees that were two hundred to three hundred years old. As they were protected by preservation laws, the new cultural center was placed on an empty area in the deepest part of the site where the old building had been located. In order for the public to notice the building, a connection to the main street was crucial. Thus, I set up a concrete frame at the boundary of the street as a roadside gallery and an entry gate to the site. It completed the entire configuration. Since the building functioned as a virtual house for exhibiting the condominiums developed by China Vanke, unaligned boxes were inserted into the main mass to differentiate the space from the real condominiums. The most important objects of the site are the old trees that bear witness to the past. The ground level where the trees are planted is lower than the level of the building and the roads, hence showing their temporal difference from the man-made. Architecture exists as the background to passing time of the old trees.

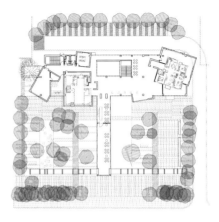

Hyunam

Gunwi, Gyeongsangbuk-do

2012

The client, who built Moheon in Daegu, launched a plan to transform 992,000m² of mountainous land in Gunwi into a natural botanical park. For a long time, the client had been transplanting and cultivating trees and observing the changes in the area. The client wanted the entire botanical garden as a space of introspection. He also wanted a small residence within the park.

The house is located in the heart of the park where only the mountains and the sky are visible. In the thick fir tree forest, five small man-made ponds were created as a prelude along the road leading to the house. Passing the ponds, you encounter a long, straight, Corten steel structure. Above it, lies a hill, and below, a valley. If you open the door, having no idea of what will happen at all, you will find nature's landscape spread out in magnificent fashion. The building connects the ground to the sky, but here, the ground disappears. There is only you, nature, and silence. Facing west, the sun sets over the reservoir in front. You come out of the house, climb the hill, and sit on the cold Corten steel chair on the silver grass. You become a part of nature. It is a time of complete solitude, a time for thought. That is why the house is named Hyunam, a humble black house.

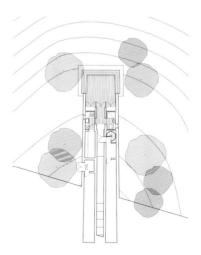

Myung Films Paju Building

Paju, Gyeonggi-do

2013

In the early 20th century, modern architects said that the basic elements of the city were residential, work, leisure, and transportation. Myung Films requested the same elements for their building. Therefore, from the beginning, it had the character of a city. To overcome the limitations of the car-centered road system, the internal pedestrian system outlined in the Paju Bookcity guidelines was actively adopted. The entire mass was divided into two parts and a wide road penetrated through the center, creating a plaza in this small building-city. A bridge and a deck connect the divided masses, making it possible to observe and respond to the events of the plaza and road. The main glass elevation towards the plaza allows the activities inside to be exposed to the exterior. The interior is more urban, with roads and small parks weaving through the various multi-purpose spaces. The building's concrete is both structure and finish. The entire process of building in concrete—the concrete workers' skill and sincerity, their acceptance and adaptation to natural conditions, and the waiting of the outcome—is like a religious ritual. Concrete is a material of high integrity, one that completely embodies the passing of time. If desired, it can be made imperishable. Myung Films is a permanent building, but its architecture is always changing.

André Bazin (1918-1958) stated that the making of a movie is a process of completing the objectivity of a moment captured in time. Myung Films exists as an ever-changing landscape. It stands firmly on the ground as an infrastructure of life. A building is not made by the architect; the residents complete it. Perhaps, much like a movie filmed by a third-party camera unintended by the director, an objective portrayal of reality created a real film and a true building. In that sense, this building is itself a city and a movie.

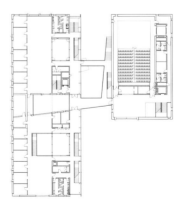

Design Vita Paju Office

Paju, Gyeonggi-do

2014

In Paju Bookcity, I had consistently argued for changing the existing road system, the greatest hurdle in the development of its first stage. Unfortunately, construction on the second stage began with the same kind of road and lot system. The second stage differed only in name —The City of Book and Film—coined from the movie industry's participation. The project site, part of the second stage of Paju Bookcity, sat on land right across from Lotte Outlet, a commercial complex that clearly did not suit the city's vision. The challenge was to make this small building maintain its presence in an area controlled by large-scale shopping.

I raised a wall on the side of the road and sought stability within. Although it was a concrete wall, I wanted to make it look like a bookshelf frame. The volume of the building, centered on a courtyard, is small in scale but filled with various things. There is a café adjacent to the communal yard, a workspace dedicated to book design, a space for exhibitions or conferences, a uniquely shaped meeting room, a small park, and a meditation area. All the spaces have different conditions of light and darkness and vary in shape and size. As they are all independent and contain different energies, a walk through this place becomes a pleasant stroll. The exterior is concrete which need not be of good-quality. Using ordinary plywood for form work, I only asked that it matched the verticality and horizontality of the elevation. It will then manifest the spirit of those who worked on its construction. Covered with a thin layer of white paint, it tells the truth.

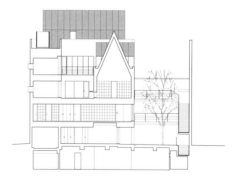

Nonsan Residence

Nonsan, Chungcheongnam-do

2014

With the relative large site area located on a steep hillside, the project sought to provide order to the imbalance of the site. Towards this end, I appropriated the distant silhouette of the towering Gyeryongsan Mountain as a mental measure for its sloped topography. It is a method that I borrowed from Dongnakdang, a house built by the Joseon Dynasty literati Lee Eonjeok who set the faraway mountains as the boundary of the house. I have learned many things from this house. Dongnakdang contains numerous large and small courtyards. Though the general principle of the Joseon noble houses was to place them on raised land at the rear of the manor grounds, its ancestral shrine was placed on the same level of the house. The shrine was, in fact, part of an intricate composition of courtyards. Even the beautiful pavilion of Gyejeong was approached as an extension of the walls that defined the courtyards. The composition of Dongnakdang was thus centered on a group of empty courtyards. Lee Eonjeok, enjoying his life of solitude within these spaces, said that he could be a rational being only through solitude.

Like Dongnakdang, the essence of the Nonsan Residence lay in the courtyards. My first move was to place the courtyards in the front, back, and center. They were then surrounded by *byeolchae* (outhouse), *haengnagchae* (quarters adjacent to the main gate), *sarangchae* (main quarters), and *anchae* (family quarters). The loose feeling of the spread-out spaces was compensated by the careful attention given to the width and height of the connecting corridors. For a more focused sense of space, each interior room was designed in the simplest of forms. The overall grouping of gable roofs was right for the sloping topography. It is pure space.

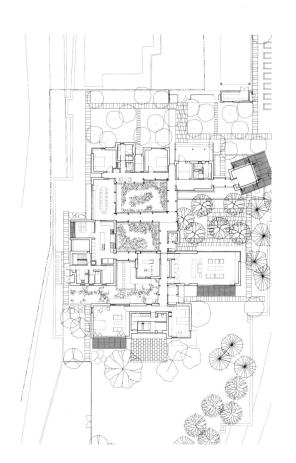

Myungrye Sacred Hill

Miryang, Gyeongsangnam-do

2015

This is a shrine dedicated to Marco Shin Seok Bok (1828-1866). An ordinary person, who sold salt and yeast, became a martyr during the Byeongin Persecution of 1866. In 1897, a small Catholic church was first built here on his birth place but was later destroyed. In 1938, a *hanok* cathedral was built in a reduced scale of the original building and is now designated as a cultural heritage. This land was originally a hill situated at the curve of Nakdong River, but now rests on dry land due to land fill. My hope is that the original landscape will be recovered at some point in the future. In addition to the cathedral, there were a few recent buildings that respected the topography of the site. The *hanok* cathedral is a humble, but meaningful and dignified structure. A new building should add to the sense of the sacred. It should be Biblical Landscape, a term that came to mind as I thought of the Woodland Cemetery.

First, to shape the entire land, I decided to build a *Via Dolorosa*, the fourteen Stations of the Cross, that are commonly depicted on the walls of a Catholic church. Using the pre-existing lots on the site, I would turn each of the fourteen Stations of the Cross into a place on the land and connect them. The final journey of this walk is completed by the water tank at the boundary of the site. The new commemorative church is built on the western slope as part of the cliff side landscape. The interior provides an experience of light and darkness and of tranquility and tension. A relatively large yard is created on the top to be used for pilgrimage events. Steps, banisters, a bell tower and other structures become part of a spatial tension. The journey from the entrance, through the Way of the Cross, to the commemorative church, and back to this yard—a long encounter with different events and scenes—constructs a road of asceticism. Through the cultivation of the road, the Biblical Landscape will be completed. The road is the most important theme of the Myungrye Sacred Hill.

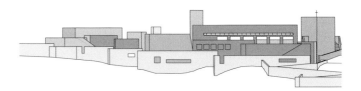

Chronological list of IROJE architecture

The year of design completion indicated.

1990 Seongbuk-dong Mr. Kang's Residence, Seoul.
Seongbuk-dong 2nd Residence, Seoul.
Central Plaza Office Building, Busan.
Clubhouse of Nada Country Club, Anseong,
Gyeonggi-do.*
1991 Suyang Building, Busan.
Clubhouse of Silk River Country Club,
Cheongju, Chungcheongbuk-do.*
1992 Youngdong Jeil Women's Hospital, Seoul.
E-mun 291, Seoul.
Sujoldang, Seoul.
1993 Daehakro Culture Center, Seoul.
Infertility Research Center of Jeil Hospital,
Seoul.
Jeil Hospital Outpatient Center Renovation,
Seoul.
1994 Dolmaru Catholic Church, Dangjin,
Chungcheongnam-do.
1995 Soonchunhyang University Library, Asan,
Chungcheongnam-do.
Soonchunhyang University Hospital Institute
of Clinical, Seoul.*
Yuldong Buddhist Temple, Gyeongju,
Gyeongsangbuk-do.*
Residence Serihun, Gapyeong, Gyeonggi-do.
1996 Yoon Women's Hospital, Guri, Gyeonggi-do.
K2 Building, Seoul.
J Women's Hospital, Cheongju,
Chungcheongbuk-do.
MizMedi Hospital, Seoul.
1997 Shin Dong Bang Ltd., Headquarters, Seoul.
Junggok-dong Church, Seoul.
Baekwoon Methodist Church, Seoul.
Sports Facility of Hyundai High School, Seoul.*
Sanbon Jeil Women's Hospital Main Building,
Gunpo, Gyeonggi-do.
Yoo Theater, Seoul.
1998 Subaekdang, Namyangju, Gyeonggi-do.
Samyoon Building Renovation, Seoul.
1999 Ganghwa Campus for Anyang University
Master Plan, Incheon.
Paju Bookcity, Paju, Gyeonggi-do.
CHA University Library, Pocheon, Gyeonggi-do.

Welcomm City, Seoul.
Samse Oriental Medical Hospital, Busan.
Saehwa Hosptial, Busan.
2000 Hansol Hospital Renovation, Seoul.
Korea National University of Arts Master Plan,
Seoul.
Sungjeong Building, Suwon, Gyeonggi-do.
Samtoh Building in Paju Bookcity, Paju,
Gyeonggi-do.*
2001 Hyehwa Culture Center of Daejeon
University, Daejeon.
Commune by the Great Wall, Badaling, Beijing,
China.
Boao Canal Village, Hainan Province, China.
CHA Hospital Extension, Seoul.*
Na & Lee Women's Hospital, Gimpo,
Gyeonggi-do.
Mirae Women's Hospital, Chuncheon,
Gangwon-do.
Dongkwang Methodist Church, Iksan,
Jeollabuk-do.
2002 Humax Village, Seongnam, Gyeonggi-do.
Sampyo Office Building Interior, Seoul.
Lock Museum, Seoul.
Vincentio Clinic, Bucheon, Gyeonggi-do.
Reed House, Yangpyeong, Gyeonggi-do.
Longhua Zhen Housing Plan, Shenzhen,
China.*
Logistic Harbor City Master Plan, Beijing,
China.
Pulmuone Lohas Academy, Goesan,
Chungcheongbuk-do.
Sunuldang, Asan, Chungcheongnam-do.
The 4.3 Peace Park Plan, Jeju-do.*
2003 Dr. Park Gallery, Yangpyeong, Gyeonggi-do.
Annex Building of Sanbon Jeil Women's
Hospital, Gunpo, Gyeonggi-do.
Gangdong Miz Women's Hospital, Seoul.
M-City Master Plan, Beijing, China.
Seocho-dong Office Building, Seoul.
Cheonan Oriental Hospital of Daejeon
University, Cheonan, Chungcheongnam-do.
2004 Kids Center of Gangseo MizMedi Hospital,

Seoul.

Dongsan Church, Ansan, Gyeonggi-do.

Sinsa-dong Building, Seoul.

Palpan-dong Residence, Seoul.

The Beautiful Store Gyeonggi Center, Paju, Gyeonggi-do.

Book Theme Park, Seongnam, Gyeonggi-do.

Changduk Palace Redevelopment Master Plan, Seoul.

Baume Couture Boutique Hotel, Jeju-do.

Monument for Mahaesong, Paju, Gyeonggi-do.

Paju Bookcity Restaurant for Workers, Paju, Gyeonggi-do.

2005   Chaowai SOHO, Beijing, China.

2nd Phase, Commune by the Great Wall, Badaling, Beijing, China.

Hyangwon Presbyterian Church, Cheorwon, Gangwon-do.

Marado Ecology Museum Master Plan, Jeju-do.*

Asia Culture Center International Design Competition, Gwangju.*

2006   Daejanggol New Town Master Plan, Hwaseong, Gyeonggi-do.*

DMZ Peace and Life Valley, Inje, Gangwon-do.

Guduk Presbyterian Church, Busan.

Maria Fertility Hospital, Seoul.

Sungman Presbyterian Church, Bucheon, Gyeonggi-do.

Eunil High School, Seoul.

Rejuvenation Design for Hwaseong Historical Cultural City, Suwon, Gyeonggi-do.*

Yeongdeungpo-gu Main Street Design, Seoul.

Yangji Housing Town Master Plan, Yongin, Gyeonggi-do.*

2007   Traditional Buddhism Culture Center of Jogye Order, Gongju, Chungcheongnam-do.

Kyobo Paju Center, Paju, Gyeonggi-do.

Artisan Building, Seoul.

Hyundai Marine and Fire Insurance Myeong-dong Office Renovation, Seoul.

Raonchae, Seoul.

Pfefferberg Museum in Berlin, Germany.*

Pavilion No.17 of Guggenheim Abu Dhabi Biennale, Abu Dhabi, Arab Emirates.*

Jindi Sihui Mixed-use Development Master Plan, Beijing, China.*

Weihai Housing Complex Master Plan, Weihai, China.*

L Creer, Seoul.

Pankyo Natural Burial Park Master Plan, Seongnam, Gyeonggi-do.*

Templestay Information Center, Seoul.

International Master Plan Competition for Multifunctional Administrative City, Sejong.*

Heonin City Development Master Plan, Seoul.*

2008   Chusa Memorial Museum, Jeju-do.

Qianmendajie Historical Area Preservation and Regeneration Plan, Beijing, China.*

Dongtan Jeil Women's Hospital, Hwaseong, Gyeonggi-do.

Jisan Waldhaus Master Plan and Housing Design, Yongin, Gyeonggi-do.

Jeju Peace Memorial Park Master Plan, Jeju-do.

30th Anniversary Memorial Building of Daejeon University, Daejeon.

L.A. Condominium Master Plan, Los Angeles, USA.*

Cheongju Central Gospels Church, Cheongju, Chungcheongbuk-do.*

2009   Earth, Water, Flower, Wind 360° Golf Clubhouse, Yeoju, Gyeonggi-do.

Moheon, Daegu.

Woojeong, Daegu.

Music Scape, Arvo Part Concert Hall International Design Competition, Tallinn, Estonia.*

Shin Dongyeop Literary Museum, Buyeo, Chungcheongnam-do.

Shaoxing Housing Complex Master Plan, Shaoxing, China.

Sentul D2 Mixed Use Complex, Kuala Lumpur, Malaysia.*

Korea Institute of Science and Technology Master Plan and L4 Design, Seoul.

Pungnam Dormitory, Seoul.

Cheongnyangni-dong Office and Community Center, Seoul.

Kyunghan Office Building, Gyeongju, Gyeongsangbuk-do.

Graveyard for President Roh Moo-hyun, Gimhae, Gyeongsangnam-do.

Toechon House, Gwangju, Gyeonggi-do.

2010   Jemunheon, Gwangju.

Seogyo-dong Neighborhood Facility, Seoul.

Jeju Alive Park Master Plan, Jeju-do.*

Foreign Language Center of Gyeongju University, Gyeongju, Gyeongsangbuk-do.*

North Gate of Korea Institute of Science and Technology, Seoul.

Yongin Residence, Yongin, Gyeonggi-do.

Mt. Odae Natural Learning Park, Pyeongchang, Gangwon-do.

Gangseo MizMedi Hospital Annex Building,
Seoul.
Pingdu Historic and Cultural Districts
Redevelopment Plan, Pingdu, China.*
2011 Chongqing Housing Complex Master Plan,
Chongqing, China.
Korean Cultural Center Austria, Wien, Austria.
Ruined Steps and May Flower, Gwangju.
Humanities Hall of Seoul National University,
Seoul.
Lotte Art Villas, Jeju-do.
Buyeo Residence, Buyeo, Chungcheongnam-
do.
Dormitory of CHA University, Pocheon,
Gyeonggi-do.
College of Pharmacy of CHA University,
Pocheon, Gyeonggi-do.
2012 Dongsoong Church's Residence, Seoul.
The Gate of Oriental Medicine Market,
Daegu.*
Yangpyeong Lock Museum, Yangpyeong,
Gyeonggi-do.*
Gampo Training Center of Gyeongju
University, Gyeongju, Gyeongsangbuk-do.*
Sangwoldae, Seoul.
Woo Jaeghil Art Museum, Gwangju.
Chungchun Church, Incheon.*
Supporting Facilities of Yeomiji Botanical
Garden, Jeju-do.
Cheonho-dong Woman Care Center, Seoul.
Daehakro Streetscape Master Plan, Seoul.
Gyeongsan Memorial Services Museum
Master Plan, Gyeongsan, Gyeongsangbuk-
do.*
Pingdu Housing Culture Center, Pingdu, China.
Lecture and Administration Hall of CHA
University, Pocheon, Gyeonggi-do.
Yongsan Park Master Plan, Seoul.
Hyunam, Gunwi, Gyeongsangbuk-do.
2013 Office Building of Samyang Chemical
Company, Seoul.
Daegu Specified Steel Sechun Factory, Daegu.
Myung Films Paju Building, Paju, Gyeonggi-do.
Solgeo Art Museum, Gyeongju,
Gyeongsangbuk-do.
Muju Residence, Muju, Jeollabuk-do.
Rium-Medi Hospital, Daejeon.
Malibu House, Los Angeles, USA.
The Source Project, Los Angeles, USA.
Huangshan Housing Complex, Huangshan,
China.
Taiyuan Wanke Center, Taiyuan, China.

2014 DMC Multiple Shopping Complex, Seoul.
Sian Memorial Park, Gwangju, Gyeonggi-do.
Hyehwa Residential College of Daejeon
University, Daejeon.
Cheonggodang, Seongnam, Gyeonggi-do.
Sageunjae, Seongnam, Gyeonggi-do.
Nonsan Residence, Nonsan,
Chungcheongnam-do.
The Tower of Pleasing Loneliness of
Gamcheon Cultural Village, Busan.
Kyung Ahm Education and Culture Foundation,
Busan.
Design Vita Paju Office, Paju, Gyeonggi-do.
Jingdezhen Project, Jingdezhen, China.
2015 Equatorial Guinea Residence, Mongomo,
Equatorial Guinea.
Myungrye Sacred Hill, Miryang,
Gyeongsangnam-do.
Tieshanping Housing Complex Master Plan,
Chongqing, China.
Youpon Project, Jiaxing, China.

* Unrealized Projects

IROJE

The meaning of IROJE, translating directly, is 'a house of stepping on dewdrops'. The origin of IROJE comes from an old Chinese Literature, *Liji* (*Record of Rites*). There was a poor living scholar who served his old father. Every early morning he used to go to the quarter where his father lived, wearing an overcoat, and waited for his father to wake up. When his father came out, the scholar handed over his warmed overcoat to his father. The way to his father's quarter was covered with dewdrops in the morning, thus the meaning of IROJE could be understood as a house for a scholar with voluntary poverty.

Seung H-Sang

Born in 1952, he graduated from Seoul National University and studied at Technische Universitaet in Wien. After working for Kim Swoo Geun for 15 years, he established his own office, 'IROJE architects & planners', in 1989. He was a core member of the '4.3 Group', which strongly influenced the Korean architectural society, and participated in founding the 'Seoul School of Architecture', a new educational system. He was a visiting professor at North London University (currently London Metropolitan University) and also taught at Seoul National University and Korea National University of Arts. He is the author of *Beauty of Poverty* (1996), *City of Wisdom, Architecture of Wisdom* (1999), *Architecture, Signs of Thoughts* (2004), *Landscript* (2009), *Graveyard for President Roh Moo-hyun* (2010), and *Old things are All Beautiful* (2012). His works are based on his critical concerns of the Western culture of the 20th century, in which the subject is the 'beauty of poverty'. He won various prizes such as the Kim Swoo Geun Culture Award and the Korean Architecture Award for his practice and works. For his participation in constructing the new city as the coordinator for 'Paju Bookcity', the America Institute of Architects invested him with the Honorary Fellowship of AIA in 2002, National Museum of Modern and Contemporary Art, Korea selected him as Artist of the Year 2002', the first time for any architect, and he held a grand solo architecture exhibition. He gained world-wide fame for his architectural achievements and various international exhibitions; his architectural field expands over Asia, Europe and America. In 2007, the Korean government honored him with the 'Korea Award for Art and Culture', and he was commissioned for the Korean Pavilion of Venice Biennale in 2008 and as director for Gwangju Design Biennale 2011. Since 2014, he, the first City Architect of Seoul Metropolitan Government, is planning and reviewing major public projects in Seoul.

Min Kyung Sik

Born in 1957, he studied at Seoul National University and received a bachelor's in Landscape Architecture and a master's in Urban Design at the Graduate School of Environmental Studies. He first began his career in architecture under Kim Swoo Geun, and then moved on to become a general manager at Space Group's New York office and the chief designer of S.O.M (Skidmore, Owings & Merrill). After opening his own firm in New York, he returned to Seoul and became a partner at Space Group. Currently, he is leading IROJE's Beijing office, established in 2008, as a partner. He is a member of AIA, KIA, and KOSID.

Lee Dong Soo

Born in 1964, he studied at the Seoul National University and joined IROJE in 1991. He became partner of the Seoul office in 2002. He taught at Korea National University of Arts from 2012 to 2014.

Kim Sung-Hee

Born in 1971, she studied at the Ulsan National University and joined IROJE in 1995. Since 2012 she is a partner of IROJE Seoul office.

IROJE People

Chronological list, current employees are in bold.

Choi Won Young, Kim Hyung Tae, Kim Kyo Jung, Jeong Bo Young, Lee Myung Jin, Kim Seung, Lee Sangjun, Ahn Yongdae, Park Byung Soon, Ahn Young Kyu, Hwang June, Lee Dongwoo, Kim Young Joon, **Lee Dong Soo**, Baek Eun Joo, Chang Yoo Kyung, Kang Dae Suk, Park Jong Youl, Lee Tae Min, Lee Jinhee, Yoo Jaewoo, Choi Sangki, Lee Ki Suk, Lee Hyung Wook, Kim Mihee, Nam Soohyun, Kim Kihwan, Kim Sungho, Ryu Jae Hyuk, **Kim Sung Hee**, Ahn Woo Sung, Park Chang Yul, Chun Young Hoon, Ko Daesuk, Yim Jae Eun, Jang Young Chul, Kang Young Pil, Kim Jong Bok, Chung Daejin, **Yun Jongtae**, Chun Sook Hee, Kim Dae Ho, **Ham Eunah**, Kim Seung Kook, Lee Kitae, Yang Hyo Jung, Yim Jinwook, Han Taeho, An Jae Hyoung, **Kim Daesun**, Choi Eun Young, Stephan Korn, Simon Guillemoz, Yim Young Mi, Park Won Dong, Sung Sangwoo, Cho Soo Young, Lee Jae Jun, Jung Hyo Won, Chung Kuho, Park Jong Hoon, Won Jungmi, Jo Jinman, Lee Younju, Lee Chul Hwan, Im

Joo Ahn, Lee Jihyun, Yum Juhyun, Sung Nayoung, Sim Hyung Keun, Oh Sewon, Jung Su Eun, Choi Won Jun, Cho Jang Eun, You Young Soo, Cho Youn Hee, Chung Sehoon, Lee Jongwon, Ham Ka Kyung, Kim Dong Wook, Kim Younji, Lee Jong Chul, Chung Jongin, Uh Hye Ryung, Park Yang Keum, Chang Hyangmi, Hwang Sunwoo, Son Yong Chan, Kwon Sook Hee, Kim Young Geun, An Jaeyoung, Cha Mijung, Chun Ka Young, Yang Hyun Jun, Lee Chang Min, Park Jooyeon, Kim Sujin, Kwon Ah Joo, Lee Jung Min, Han Junghan, Cha Seung Yeon, Lee Kyoung Jae, Kwon Soonwoo, Park Joo Hee, Lee Moon Ho, Oh Hyogyeong, Kang Hyemi, **Choi Hyeon**, Yoon Kyungsup, Son Nam Young, Lee Donghee, Choi Keun Suk, **Han Gui Hua**, Kim Yehwon, Jin Youngkwan, Kwak Dong Hyun, Yoon Bohyun, Yoon Gwangjae, Lee Hyae Won, Kim Inhan, Liang Fei, Joo Sung Suk, Fu Xin, Lee Min Jung, **Shin Joongsu**, Kwon Miseon, Kim Tae Beom, Matthew Whittaker Lawrence Charles, Han Sinwook, Cui GuangMing, Sun ZhiJun, **Kim Tae Yong**, **Xu LianHua**, Kim Kihyun, Go Eunbi, **Lee Wansun**, Choi Joong Churl, Na Kyeong-eun, Min So Jung, Kim Bokyeon, Tian Hui, Kim Seonju, Chu Yoon Jung, Clayton Strange Charles, **Lee Go Eun**, Kim Sehyeon, Kim Zyi Ryong, Winiewicz Filip Rafal, Peng KaiNing, Jung Solmin, **Pyo Ha Rim**, Son Junsik, Kim Sanghyo, **Kim Sunyeop**, Wada Tsuyoshi, Shin Hyunkook, **Lee Kyubin**, Kim Soyeon, Hong Jonghwa, **Kim Kee Won**, **Lee Joong Hyun**, Ahn Youjin, Jang Yujin, **Lee Kye Hyeon**, **Go Il Hwan**, Xu Ying, Dolmans Frederik Willem, Zheng SaiSai, Pei YuFei, Jia Mo, Kwon Soo Jung, Ha Sang Jun, Jung Woo Yeoll, **Oh Eunju**, Jacob Kalmakoff, Shin Yeung, Hwang Hyosung, **Pee Yejun**, **Yoon Soon Hyuk**, **Lee Jaemin**, Robert Joseph James Huges, **Zhao TaiHao**, **Lee SeungHee**, **Lee ChangHyun**, Yu Chen, **An JinHo**, **Cha Hye Rhan**, **Lee Sangjun**, Zuo JiaNing, **Choi Jiwoo**, **Wu TongYu**, **Kim Esther Tammy**, **Eom Ki Beom**, **Choi Bora**, **Hwang Namin**, **Hyun Eunsoo**

Seung H-Sang Document © 2016 by Seung H-Sang
Co-published by Youlhwadang Publishers and
Architectural Publisher B

Editors: Yi Soojung, Bak Mi
Designer: Bak Soyoung

Youlhwadang Publishers
Gwanginsa-gil 25, Paju-si, Gyeonggi-do, Korea
Tel +82-31-955-7000 Fax +82-31-955-7010
www.youlhwadang.co.kr yhdp@youlhwadang.co.kr

Architectural Publisher **B**
William Wains gade 9
1432 Copenhagen K. Denmark
www.b-arki.dk gilberthansen@b-arki.dk

ISBN (Youlhwadang) 978-89-301-0514-9
ISBN (Architectural Publisher B) 978-87-92700-13-1

Printed in Korea

A CIP catalogue record of the National Library of Korea for this
book is available at the homepage of CIP(http://seoji.nl.go.kr) and
Korean Library Information System Network(http://www.nl.go.kr/
kolisnet). (CIP2016003788).